Emma is walking to school friend Pat.
They pass the old antique shop.
There is something in the window that catches her eye.
"Wait a minute, Pat," she says.

There's a small silver box in the window. It is shiny and has the most beautiful pattern on the lid.

"How much is it?" asks Pat.

"It doesn't say," says Emma, "but I'm going to buy it... somehow."

"Don't be daft!" says Pat. "It will cost a fortune."

"I'll save up," says Emma.

Emma thinks about the silver box all day.

She has £30 saved up at home.

Her 18th birthday is coming up soon.

Her gran and her two aunties always give her money.

And she will save all the money her mum gives her every week...

Every day Emma and Pat check the silver box is still there.

"You need to know how much it costs," says Pat. "Go in and ask!"

They look through the window.

A man is standing in the shop.

He is looking at them. Scary!

"I'll have enough money," says Emma. "It's my birthday soon."

But one day the silver box isn't there.
Emma looks at every shelf in the window.
She can't believe it. Someone has
bought it!
It's so unfair.

In the classroom, Emma starts to cry. Mrs Day, her teacher, is worried.

"Whatever is the matter?" she asks.

"It's… it's… the silver box!" sobs Emma. "It's my birthday on Friday. I was going to buy it with my savings and birthday money. But it's gone."

"Maybe the shopkeeper has just moved it?" says Mrs Day.

"No, it's been sold," sobs Emma. "I know it has."

It's Friday and it's Emma's birthday. She comes downstairs and opens her presents.

She has lots of cards and a few small presents. But there's no money. There is just Mum's present left. It feels like a small cardboard box. She starts to open it.

It's the silver box!

Emma can hardly believe it.

Inside there is a necklace with earrings that match.

"Those belonged to your great-gran," her mum says. "She passed them on to Gran. Then Gran gave them to me."

"Now that you're 18 I'm giving them to you. You must take very good care of them."

"Oh, I will! Oh, thank you!" says Emma.

"Gran and your aunties helped to pay for the box," says Mum. "You must thank them, too."

"I will!" Emma says.

"How did you know about the silver box?" asks Emma.

Mum is smiling. "Pat told me," she says.

"Well, the necklace, the earrings, the silver box…

they're the best present… ever!" says Emma.